PRAISE FOR L.M. BROWNING

"This generation's New England Transcendalist."
— Frank Owen, creator of Bodhiyatra Poetry

"L.M. Browning's religious fervor reminds one of Emily Dickinson's in its intensity and unorthodoxy: it bypasses dogma to reach the heart of the divine."
—Rennie McQuilkin, Author of *The Weathering*

"L.M.'s potent verse gently takes our hand and asks us to leave our desks. To leave the familiar. To step out of the tiresome false asphalt roads and onto the wooded trails and soft moist knowingness that resides in our hearts. There is revelation in her suffering prose, in her darkness, and her failures. In her willingness and courage. The words pour out of her fingers. She is, in a way, deeply connected to the source of suffering and to the root of our human condition. She is not afraid to look the many elements of our mortal life and to transcend them with fierce belief in the ancient ways."
—Alan Cooke, Emmy-winning writer and filmmaker

"L.M. Browning's powerful poetry embodies the archetypal spiritual journey of our times, from "confining doctrine," through despair and doubt, into reverent reconnection with the mysteries of the blossoming world. Her impassioned words evoke our longing to unite with the Source that gave rise to the cosmos, the earth, and the depths of our hearts. This book is like holding the twilight in your hands: a luminous joining of the divine and the natural into a moment of sacred wonder!"
—Drew Dellinger, author of *Love Letter to the Milky Way*

"Browning's poems are of exquisite quality. Like all excellent poetry, no modifier, no imagery, no reference is gratuitous. Ms Browning's literary background is not only impressive, it is aesthetically set to reinforce and construct a world of rich imagery."
—Jean-Yves Vincent Solinga,
  author of *Clair-Obscur of the Soul*

Vagabonds and Sundries

POETIC REMANANTS OF LIVES PAST

Vagabonds and Sundries

POETIC REMANANTS OF LIVES PAST

L.M. BROWNING

HOMEBOUND
PUBLICATIONS
Independent Publisher of Contemplative Titles
STONINGTON, CONNECTICUT

PUBLISHED BY HOMEBOUND PUBLICATIONS

Copyright © 2013 by L.M. Browning. All Rights Reserved. Without limiting the rights under copyright reserved above, no part of this publication may be reproduced, stored in or introduced into a retrieval system or transmitted in any means (electronic, mechanical, photocopying, recording or otherwise) without the prior written permission of both the copyright owner and publisher. Except for brief quotations embodied in critical articles and reviews.

Homebound Publications books may be purchased for educational, business, or sales promotional use. For information please write: Special Markets Department, Homebound Publications, PO Box 1442, Pawcatuck, CT 06379

Visit us www.homeboundpublications.com
or visit the author at www.lmbrowning.com

FIRST EDITION HARDCOVER

ISBN: 978-1-938846-28-1
Book Designed by Leslie M. Browning
Cover Images by © Sundari | Shutterstock.com

Library of Congress Cataloging-in-Publication Data

Browning, L. M.
 [Poems. Selections]
 Vagabonds and Sundries : Poetic Remanants of Lives Past / by L.M. Browning. —First edition.
    pages cm
 ISBN 978-1-938846-28-1 (hardcover)
 I. Title.
 PS3602.R738A6 2013
 811'.6—dc23
                                                                    2013035782

10 9 8 7 6 5 4 3 2 1

Homebound Publications holds a fervor for environmental conservation. Atop donating a percentage of our annual income to an ecological charity, we are ever-mindful of our "carbon footprint". Our books are printed on paper with chain of custody certification from the Forest Stewardship Council, Sustainable Forestry Initiative, and the Programme for the Endorsement of Forest Certification. This ensures that, in every step of the process, from the tree to the reader's hands, that the paper our books are printed on has come from sustainably managed forests.

ALSO BY L.M. BROWNING

POETRY

Ruminations at Twilight: Poetry Exploring the Sacred
Oak Wise: Poetry Exploring an Ecological Faith
The Barren Plain: Poetry Exploring the Reality of the Modern Wasteland
Fleeting Moments of Fierce Clarity: Journal of a New England Poet
Vagabonds and Sundries: Poetic Remnants of Lives Past

FICTION

The Nameless Man

The joy I carry with me;
while all the pain I have come to terms with
is bound here between two covers
and left as a sundry along the roadside.

CONTENTS

Sundries	1
Primal	2
The Quelling	3
Ashes, Dust, and Air	4
Respite	5
Put Upon the Pyre	6
Eating the Poison	7
Disarticulation of Life and Peace	9
Lover from Another Life	10
The Cannibalistic Kind	11
Meet the Dawn	12
August 15, 1998	13
The Tides Driving Against the Seawalls	14
Down Along the River Styx	15
The Organic Body of Memory	16
That Afternoon in the Cafe	18
My Body of Work	19
Unwanted Bedfellows	20
Immortal Beloved	22
Our Paradox	24
The Familiar Mystery	25
The Writer's Confession	26
The Amused Derision of an Indifferent God	27

Measures of Devotion	28
Hardened	29
Metamorphosis	30
My Flesh and Blood	31
Dormant Answers	32
My Religion Is New England	34
To Know the Unknowable	36
The Sum of the Parts	37
Sacrifice the Future to Survive the Present	38
The Greatest Deception Ever Sold	39
Choices Scarcely Recalled	40
Deep Notes, Quick Pace	41
Simplicity	43
The Boat-Rocker	44
During the Long Day, Over the Sacred Night	46
The Tempest	49
The Lament of the Wayfarer	51

About the Author

About the Press

"I have a deeply hidden and
inarticulate desire for something
beyond the daily life."
—Virgina Woolf

"Believe in a love that is being stored up for you
like an inheritance, and have faith that
in this love there is a strength and a blessing so
large that you can travel as far as you wish
without having to step outside it."
—Rainer Maria Rilke, *Letters to a Young Poet*

"There will come a time when everybody will know why,
for what purpose, there is all this suffering, and there will be
no more mysteries. But now we must live."
— Anton Chekhov, *The Three Sisters*

Sundries

On that day
When my ashes
Are scattered
Unto the winds

Regather my soul
And carry me with you
Across the breadth
Of your days

My words in hand,
My vision in heart,
The leaves of my days
Bound between two covers.

Primal

Bring up the tribal drums
This life has become a procession
—All of us walking unto the dark horizon.
The symphony of life
Is but a dirge.

Ride the descent bold and fiery.
Scream fiercely and love tenderly
Before the darkness engulfs.

The Quelling

Within your silence, Demon
I hear your surrender.

As you go to your end
And I celebrate my beginning,

We come the inevitable outcome
Wherein we—both of us—

Reap what we have sown.

This spirit you have starved
Is nourished by the fruition
Of long-held hopes you resented.

And your ego, made fat
By your exploitation of others,
Must learn how to sustain itself.

My life, now reclaimed,
Is no longer your feast.

Ashes, Dust, and Air

And in that moment
I saw
The beginning,
Middle
And end

And surrendered myself
To the climb,
The leap
And the fall
We all must take.

Respite

Bow taken,
Sun set,
Door shut,
Behind the curtain drawn,

I exhale.

Put Upon the Pyre

What can you hold over me
When I no longer fear the end?

How will you hold me
Now that I know how weak you are?

You doled everything out in drops
To keep me coming on my knees.

Until the day when I knew
I'd rather starve than beg.

I'd rather wrap myself in rags
Than whore myself for your secondhand silks.

I'd rather wander alone
Than have you drag me any further.

I burned my bridges
So the devil couldn't follow.

Eating the Poison

I tried to give you love
But you wanted none of it.

You won't respect the terms
Of our parting.

Sadly, my hate is the strongest emotion
Ever shown for you.

You live off my disgust now,
Just as you once fed on my hopes.

Disgraced and feeble as you are
This fight is all you have.

Yet I know how to end
The unending cycle.

I leave the heirloom memories along
The roadside—sundries from an old life.

If I hold no hate for you
And give no thought to you

This prolonged game
Comes to its close.

You will go to your chosen fate
And I shall go to mine.

Disarticulation of Life and Peace

There is no time to think.
The age of never-ending duties has dawned.

As a child I knew what it was
To be alone with my thoughts.

And not be pulled at by
Alerts, notices, invites, and likes.

Focus split six ways,
We haven't the ability to concentrate.

We are never settled,
Never alone.

Never give ourselves fully
Or receive each other's undivided attention.

Being connected to everything
Has disconnected us from ourselves
And the preciousness of this present moment.

Lover from Another Life

You are the one I've spent my life with.
No, not the one I married,
Not the one I wake up with,
But the one I've gone to bed with.

Thoughts of you
    —Of the one day we spent together
    Suspended in serendipity and intensity—
Sustain me through the hours spent
Staring up at the ceiling through the darkness,
The tedium of the years pulling at my soul.

In a parallel life,
Without trains beckoning, obligations waiting
And circumstances dictating,
Our ghosts still roaming the city streets—
Living out the life we couldn't have.

The Cannibalistic Kind

Walking with you
Through the moonlight
During my darkest day
I can see it now:

> The heavy shadows of demons
> Cling to your heels
> Stretching their wings in your wake,
> Threatening my peace.

You think me naive and gullible
But I have looked past your skin
And down the years into your future.

There shall come a day
When you will be taken in by one
With an illusion more elaborate than your own
And you will be fed
Your own silver tongue.

Meet the Dawn

The tonic
For the weary soul
Steeps in the waning moonlight
And is poured out in a flood
At sunrise.

August 15, 1998

On one warm August night,
As I lay sleeping
My father woke me
And began telling me
A story of the world.

The brothers and sisters
I would have known
Had he not died
Sitting by his side.

The Tides Driving Against the Seawalls

The doldrums of this gray village
Can weigh or sooth.

Embanked behind the fog,
I meander the narrow slate sidewalks
Towards the point
Where I know the gales
Will drown out that voice telling me
    All I must do,
    All I should do,
    All I could have done.

I'll sit on the storm walls
And watch with blank mind
The slow path of the trawlers
Looking sympathetically upon them,
The chipped paint shedding from their hulls
And rusted joints bleeding red,
Knowing they know what it is
To weather the world.

Down Along the River Styx

Wrapped in your straightjacket of self-involvement
We plow ahead into the dark horizon
Conjured by your ill-yearnings.

You built this faulty ship
With its warped compass and missing keel,
With its brittle bones and gutted sails.

You set the course to that forsaken place
And hold to it each day no matter my pleas
And the omens warning you away.

Why must I make the journey unto ruin with you?
You do not value my companionship.
You simply want company in your misery.

You do not care how many years I lose,
Never taking into account what I might have wanted.

The only need you have of me is as a nursemaid
When at last this boat runs aground
And the vulturous society you keep comes to eat you alive.

...And you curse me for jumping ship.

The Organic Body of Memory

The vibrancy of my life
Decays into the husks
Of these words.

I have nothing to bequeath to you
But the faint shadows
Of bright moments
Never to be recaptured.

Try as I may
To resuscitate what has been
With words

The defining moments
Lived by one, in full,
Cannot be imparted to another.

Even I, the one who has lived this life
Hardly remember
A fraction of what I have
Known, felt and faced.

Traces of these moments
Course in my blood
And lend color to my soul.

But they are no longer recollections
To be shared
They are this individual
You may explore
But will never wholly understand.

That Afternoon in the Cafe

Mouth and hands tied
By the life I've already chosen.

Sitting silently across from you
Railing against all that my lips wants to say
And all my hands long to do.

Firmly beset, utterly bewitched,
Not free to go forward
Yet incapable of simply forgetting you
And return to life as it was.

Unwilling to meet your eyes,
Knowing that you see into me
Hearing all that goes unspoken.

I sit clutching my heavy mug of cooling tea,
Biting my lip, lost in a struggle
Waiting for you to tell me
Where we'll go from here.

My Body of Work

While these pages may seem
Bleach white in color
They are not.

They are soaked with the blood
That seeped from my wounds
During the nights
Of my demons' feasts.

While these pages may seem
Molded from wooden pulp
They are not.

The velum
Is stretched from my own skin
And the spine woven
With the hair that fell out
Over the long nights of fear and worry.

You hold an embodiment of the wound,
My last ditch effort to drain the infection
And make way for new growth.

Unwanted Bedfellows

I live in a house
Filled with ghosts.

The cat sees them,
Waking from a dead sleep
To stare out into the emptiness
Where the demons dance, disembodied.

I used to see them,
When I was a child,
Unaccustomed to being haunted.

Their presence now common,
They blend into the backdrop
Of the pale white walls.

Resigned that I shall never
Be rid of these dark bedfellows,
Each night, I crawl into bed
With the jilted figures
Of the inescapable ill memories

Staring out into the black,
Longing for comfort
Which seems only a transient
—Coming unexpectedly,
Always to leave.

Immortal Beloved

We have the power
To remove each other
From the monotony of the days.

We rotate around one another
—Pulling each other
Into a gulf
Where magic endures.

Colliding
Every few years
For a handful of stolen hours
We spend bewitched and blissful.

Tempted to merge our two lives,
We cannot create something new
Without destroying what we have now.

This singular love,
Out lives lovers and friend.
Why ground ourselves?
Why bring each other
Down to earth to share the mundane?

When we could live together
For a lifetime
Suspended immortal
In a womb removed from daily duties
Where we two outcasts
Can give each other solace.

Our Paradox

You wild thing
Your spontaneity is what pulls me toward you
And what drives me away.

It is what makes a single night surreally blissful
And a life-long impossible.

For, after the rush,
I require the calm.

We yearn for the transient
But require the balance of what is settled
If we are to flourish.

The Familiar Mystery

Within the muddle of influences
I listen for my voice.
Extracting myself from all that I was taught
So to be free to remember what I knew.

Do we ever see our own face?
Wipe off the thick make-up of parody
So to be free to see the stunning authenticity.

To think, we might live a lifetime in this skin
But never know who we are.

This Writer's Confession

I have lived on words for fifteen years
They've been my religion—
The unexhausted basket of bread
From which I draw each day.

Yet a part of me is starved.

I dig deep into the souls of my lovers and friends
Until I hit bone, still unsatisfied.

The marrow I seek is meaning,
Sweet, intoxicating, nourishing.

In my youth, I said I would rather starve
Than eat the bitterness of shallow pleasantries.

But that was a declaration of a youth,
Unscathed, undiminished, unburdened.

And the daily yields have been bitter for some time.

Do we have the right to voice our unhappiness
If we have not the will to change what is making us ill?

The Amused Derision of an Indifferent God

We sit
Sprawled out on the floor,
Children fighting with puzzle pieces
That won't fit together.

Not knowing
The greater picture
The fragments of truth will make,

Going unaided
By a God who prefers
To watch us scurry.

Measures of Devotion

The fruits of the years
Are not shown
In the certainties gathered
But in the lengths we have gone
In our search for understanding.

When all faith has gone
And the lines of the self blur into gray
The journey is our testament.

Hardened

I am acquainted with the night,
Acclimated to the dark.
So much so, that the light
Is now a stranger
And ease, foreign.

Metamorphosis

There will come a day,
Years away from this

Where I shall take into my own hands
This, my life

   —A journey that only I can know
   The full depth and breadth of—

And upon my own terms
Start the next leg of the path

With only this suffocated soul
And the few things I know to be true
Making the transition.

Only I know what the hours have been
Only I can appreciated the significance
Of the full circle
Coming from beginning to end.

My Flesh and Blood

My ghosts rattle through the house,
The same now, as they did decades ago
Upon the nights of their creation.

Once tormenting me with the memories they carry,
I have grown accustom to their presence,
Tending them as if they were my children,

Rather than my captors.

Once I laid awake trying to undo them.
Now I sit with them, tending to their survival,
Afraid of what life would be without their company.

Dormant Answers

I sat for a time
By the burning bush.
A naked child
Among the harsh winds
Yet, while the flames were high,
They gave no warmth.

I sat for a time
At the foot of the mountain
Waiting for the prophet to descend,
In need of understanding
Only to find, I wanted to live the truth
Not receive it secondhand.

I sat for a time
Outside of the tomb
Waiting for love to be resurrected
That I might be healed.
Only to learn, what has past
Never returns exactly as it was.

I sat for a time
Among monks draped in maroon and saffron robes

That I might understand my suffering
And come to terms with the nature of our existence.
Only to admit that I could not concede
Life is meant to be pain.

All this I did that I might learn.
Yet am left knowing less now
Than I did when I set out.

Coming to see,
That we need not seek.
We need only find those things
That help us remember.

My Religion Is New England

My feast days come
When the apples are ripe
And the blueberries
Hang heavy with juice.

My communal wine
Is the crisp salty liquor sipped
From the oysters that grow
Along the black rocks in the bays.

On the afternoons when the molted leaves
Float in the air like bronzed snow flakes
And the gnarled pumpkin patches
Yield their copper bounty.

Walking across the wide floor boards,
Parched gray with dust,
Bending for the low horse-hair plaster ceilings,
Following the cramped stairways leading up to bed.

When the smell of the smoldering hearth
Beckons me home
As I walk through the village
On the first chilled winter night.

Having a heavy mug of hot cider,
A bowl of hearty fish stew.
And watch the fishing boats come in at dusk,
Their hulls loaded down heavy.

Sitting from my place along the shore,
Looking out unto tall masts,
The smell of the brine
When the wind is high in the east.

Driving down wooded roads,
Following the unending thread of stonewalls,
Winding along beneath the bower
Of Oaks, Maples, and Walnut trees.

I find that my home is my church.
And my heaven, a chair by the hearth.

In the dearness of it,
I find the sacred at work.

In partaking of it
—Belonging to it—
My heart swells
With a joy not to be conveyed.

To Know the Unknowable

We stretch ourselves
To bring the ineffable into words
In our desire to hold that which is spirit
And to know that which is boundless.

The Sum of the Parts

I once called myself
A Christian, then a Jew,
Then a Buddhist, then a Muslim,

But that was in the beginning
When I regarded my search for God
As a portion of my life
Rather than life itself.

Sacrifice the Future to Survive the Present

The body thirsts for water,
The heart for love,
And the soul for transcendence.

Left unfulfilled,
The hungers turn inward
And self-consuming.

Undernourished,
We are left letting your own blood
To fill our cup.
Until that day
When we take too much.

The Greatest Deception Ever Sold

For millennia
God has been a bestseller.

His work has been sold,
His image has been sold,
His blessing, his salvation.

And yet,
For all the money we have paid
To the hawkers of doctrine,
We have gained no understanding.

We have been sold an idea;
While the man himself
Brushed past us
Among the crowded market.

Choices Scarcely Recalled

The dark molasses passing of time
During those days when I cannot recall
What I have achieved
And can think of nothing else
I am tempted to pursue.

In my youth I spoke with God
During the confluence of night and dawn.
He has since wandered off
To tend to unknown matters
Leaving me to mutter to myself.

I cannot recall how long I have sat here
Waiting for his return,
Raging at him as the years lapse.

Only to realize that it was I
Who left the conversation
To tend to a million little things
That never needed my attention.

Deep Notes, Quick Pace

The despairing beauty of the music
Causes us to lament life as we live it.

The capture and loss of the moment
   —The bittersweet quality
     Of these fleeting days—
Deepen the significance of what is felt.

The fragility of time
  —Strong one moment,
    Fading the next—
Is the seduction
Of the human experience.

The momentary ripeness of this flesh,
The short space of this breath,
Quickly withered,
The beauty is missed
If not lived.

Each note
Sweet and somber
Has its harmony.

This movement
Rushes so quickly
Unto silence.

Fall backward
Into the tide.
Be carried away.

Simplicity

There are days when
Life is complex
And I require some answer
To the hows and whys
That surround the mysterious forces
At work in my life.

And still there are days
When life is simple
And all I need is a heavy coat
To wrap around me,
A sturdy pair of boots,
And a bag big enough
To carry my load.

Those days when
Our suffering recedes,
The gray curtain rolls back,
And the beauty of what it is to draw breath
        Pervades.

The Boat-Rocker

I overturned
The boat once
And nearly drowned.

Coughing up
The heavy waters
I choked upon,
I lay limp.

Rescued,
Part of me died
In the storm.

Gasping, the defiant self
   Was the victim
And the pragmatist
   The survivor.

A boat-rocker once,
I am left to fear
The open waters,

Stranded on
The barren island

To which my trauma
Confines me.

I stand quietly screaming,
Yearning for cause
To revive the wild ways,
To take a stand as I once did—
    Fearless and fierce amidst churning swells.

During the Long Day, Over the Sacred Night

I lost myself
Somewhere between
The dawn and dusk.

Somewhere,
In serving you
I lost my self-worth.

Somewhere,
In trying to survive
I sold what gave the days meaning.

Somewhere,
In seeking the truth
I discovered the extent of lies.

Somewhere,
While needing your love
I altered myself to gain embrace.

Somewhere,
In needing to believe,
I let myself be deceived.

Somewhere,
While telling my story to you
Your fictions became my biology.

Yet somewhere,
Sometime...somehow
I found myself
There, in-between
Sunset and sunrise.

There,
In the dark,
When your light
Was no longer upon me,
I could see myself.

There,
In the silence
That opened while you slept,
I could hear myself.

There,
In the solitude,

Detoxified of that need for your touch,
I could feel myself.

There,
In the gulf between worlds
Where body and being are in harmony,
I remembered the whole of what I am.

There,
In the absence of desperation,
I gave myself the freedom to be
And came to love what lies within.

The Tempest

Life: A period of years that passes in the space of a breath, during which we become all things.

Birth unto death is a fiery ride from the light of first dawn through the blackest night. The heart of history beats and in that space of a moment we are born, live, die, and come to dust. Through this human condition, we are sent naked into a world of violent experience. For one fierce fleeting moment—during the flash of this single life—we are all things: We are passion; we are need; we are desire; we are gratitude; we are despair; we are hope; we are transcendence; we are rage and reckless abandon; we are hunger and we are fullness.

Through this life—the duration of this body—we take voice and express the pent-up needs and agonies of our mute soul. Alive we burn with fervor—self-consuming—mortals demanding answers of the god.

Transient spirits passing briefly through this body, for a short time we can reach out to another—bind ourselves to another; lose ourselves and find ourselves; cower in shame and stand in pride; feel the grip of deepest love and burn till the new dawn extinguishes the night.

Some are undone by the moment, unable to bear the neck-breaking swings from happiness into desolation. This fleeting moment of beauty is so profound, we grieve when we reflect on it. This moment of joy, need, curiosity, and loneliness is so entrancing that we forget we are experiencing it all in a free-fall.

Even the most desperate pain—the most terrifying madness—has a sweetness; for in feeling, we know what it is to be human.

Enduring the tempest, naked amid the surging elements—this is life. To be vulnerable and afraid; lost and longing for home, lying in need of some other from who we may draw strength. In the torrent of experience we are swept up into the currents of emotion, left grasping at each other for some anchor, else we be carried off.

As with any fleeting moment, the sweetness is in the sorrow and the sorrow in the sweetness. The moment comes, it fills us, we are alight with it, and then...it is gone.

The Lament of the Wayfarer

When the day comes
And I at last clear this dense wood,
I shall meet you on the other side.

When the day comes
And my path comes back to the place it began,
We shall go on to that next place together.

When the dawn comes to this night
And I have seen you through the worst,
You will sit with me until I close my eyes
And I wake in my bed,
In that home I left so long ago.

When the day comes
And I can at last pull up
The moorings holding my soul in place,
I shall journey to you
And set fire to this vessel I dwell in

Never to leave you again.

ABOUT THE AUTHOR

L.M. Browning grew up in a small fishing village in Connecticut. A longtime student of religion, nature, art, and philosophy these themes permeate her work. She is the author of a three-title contemplative poetry series: *Ruminations at Twilight, Oak Wise,* and *The Barren Plain*. These three books went on to garner several accolades including a total of 3 pushcart-prize nominations and the Nautilus Gold Medal for Poetry.

Balancing her passion for writing with her love of education and publishing, Browning is a graduate of the University of London and a Fellow with the League of Conservationist Writers. She is partner at Hiraeth Press; Co-Founder of *Written River: A Journal of Eco-Poetics* as well as Founder of *The Wayfarer: A Journal of Contemplative Literature*. In 2011, Browning opened Homebound Publications—a rising independent publishing house based in New England.

In 2012 she released *Fleeting Moments of Fierce Clarity: Journal of a New England Poet*. It went on to be named a finalist in the Next Generation Indie Book Awards. The book is a combination journal and poetry collection following her daily contemplative life and her travels throughout New England. In summer 2013, she followed up this success with the release of her first full-length novel, *The Nameless Man*.

She currently divides her time between her home in Connecticut and her work in Boston.

www.lmbrowning.com

HOMEBOUND
PUBLICATIONS

AT HOMEBOUND PUBLICATIONS WE RECOGNIZE THE IMPORTANCE of going home to gather from the stores of old wisdom to help nourish our lives in this modern era. We choose to lend voice to those individuals who endeavor to translate the old truths into new context and keep alive through the written word ways of life that are now endangered. Our titles introduce insights concerning mankind's present internal, social and ecological dilemmas.

It is our intention at Homebound Publications to revive contemplative storytelling. We publish full-length introspective works of: non-fiction, essay collections, epic verse, short story collections, journals, travel writing, and novels. In our fiction titles our intention is to introduce new perspectives that will directly aid mankind in the trials we face at present.

It is our belief that the stories humanity lives by give both context and perspective to our lives. Some older stories, while well-known to the generations, no longer resonate with the heart of the modern man nor do they address the present situation we face individually and as a global village. Homebound chooses titles that balance a reverence for the old sensibilities; while at the same time presenting new perspectives by which to live.

WWW.HOMEBOUNDPUBLICATIONS.COM

CPSIA information can be obtained at www.ICGtesting.com
Printed in the USA
LVOW06*0638101013

356311LV00001B/1/P

9 781938 846281